1 & 2

TIMOTHY

Living Out the Gospel

LOVEGODGREATLY.COM

AT LOVE GOD GREATLY, YOU'LL FIND
REAL, AUTHENTIC WOMEN. WOMEN WHO
ARE IMPERFECT, YET FORGIVEN.

Women who desire less of us, and a whole lot
more of Jesus. Women who long to know God
through his Word, because we know that Truth
transforms and sets us free. Women who are
better together, saturated in God's Word and in
community with one another.

Welcome, friend. We're so glad you're here...

CONTENTS

WELCOME

We are glad you have decided to join us in this Bible study! First of all, please know that you have been prayed for! It is not a coincidence you are participating in this study.

Our prayer for you is simple: that you will grow closer to our Lord as you dig into His Word each and every day! As you develop the discipline of being in God's Word on a daily basis, our prayer is that you will fall in love with Him even more as you spend time reading from the Bible.

Each day before you read the assigned scripture(s), pray and ask God to help you understand it. Invite Him to speak to you through His Word. Then listen. It's His job to speak to you, and it's your job to listen and obey.

Take time to read the verses over and over again. We are told in Proverbs to search and you will find: "Search for it like silver, and hunt for it like hidden treasure. Then you will understand" (Prov. 2:4–5 NCV).

All of us here at Love God Greatly can't wait for you to get started, and we hope to see you at the finish line. Endure, persevere, press on—and don't give up! Finish well what you are beginning today. We will be here every step of the way, cheering you on! We are in this together. Fight to rise early, to push back the stress of the day, to sit alone and spend time in God's Word! Let's see what God has in store for you in this study! Journey with us as we learn to love God greatly with our lives!

As you go through this study, join us in the following resources below:

Weekly Blog Posts •

Weekly Memory Verses •

Weekly Monday Videos •

Weekly Challenges •

Facebook, Twitter, Instagram •

LoveGodGreatly.com •

Hashtags: #LoveGodGreatly •

RESOURCES

Join Us

ONLINE
lovegodgreatly.com

STORE
lovegodgreatly.com/store

FACEBOOK
facebook.com/LoveGodGreatly

INSTAGRAM
instagram.com/lovegodgreatlyofficial

TWITTER
@_LoveGodGreatly

DOWNLOAD THE APP

CONTACT US
info@lovegodgreatly.com

CONNECT
#LoveGodGreatly

LOVE
GOD
GREATLY

Love God Greatly (LGG) is a beautiful community of women who use a variety of technology platforms to keep each other accountable in God's Word. We start with a simple Bible reading plan, but it doesn't stop there.

Some women gather in homes and churches locally, while others connect online with women across the globe. Whatever the method, we lovingly lock arms and unite for this purpose: to love God greatly with our lives.

In today's fast-paced technology-driven world, it would be easy to study God's Word in an isolated environment that lacks encouragement or support, but that isn't the intention here at Love God Greatly. God created us to live in community with Him and with those around us.

Would you consider reaching out and doing this study with someone?

We need each other, and we live life better together. Because of this, would you consider reaching out and doing this study with someone?

Rest assured we'll be studying right alongside you—learning with you, cheering for you, enjoying sweet fellowship, and smiling from ear to ear as we watch God unite women together—intentionally connecting hearts and minds for His glory.

So here's the challenge: call your mom, your sister, your grandma, the girl across the street, or the college friend across the country. Gather a group of girls from your church or workplace, or meet in a coffee shop with friends you have always wished you knew better.

Arm-in-arm and hand-in-hand, let's do this thing... together.

LGG SPANISH TESTIMONY

ESTHER, SPAIN

When I started the Love God Greatly Ruth study I felt empty, as if my soul and emotions were in a desert. I had been spiritually abused and had lost my trust in Christian leadership. I was filled with discouragement and frustration. I couldn't worship.

The Lord surprised me on the very first day of the study when my group facilitator explained that she was there to learn alongside all of us. It was beautiful how we were all learning from each other. We were all disciples. As the study went on and I started to read what my sisters shared, the wall of protection I had built around me began to fall down. I felt that God was rescuing me from the bottom of the sea where I was drowning. I felt like I was breathing again and God was telling me, "There are people who love me and crave to fill up with My Word." That day I started to cry as God began to heal my broken heart.

Now I want to read my Bible again, I want to pray, and I want to worship like never before. I crave to know God more and to live a new life. Even my husband is changing and healing from being exposed to God's Word!

I can't thank Love God Greatly enough for making these studies available to us. Your work is not in vain!

Thank you, Jesus.

I felt that God was rescuing me from the bottom of the sea where I was drowning.

To connect with LGG Spanish Branch:

- Site: AmaaDiosGrandemente.com
- Facebook page: Ama a Dios Grandemente
- Pinterest: pinterest.com/AmaaDios
- Instagram: instagram.com/amaadiosgrandemente

Do you know someone who could use our Love God Greatly Bible studies in Spanish? If so, make sure and tell them about LGG Spanish and all the amazing Bible study resources we provide to help equip them with God's Word!!!

SOAP STUDY

HOW AND WHY TO SOAP

In this study we offer you a study journal to accompany the verses we are reading. This journal is designed to help you interact with God's Word and learn to dig deeper, encouraging you to slow down and reflect on what God is saying to you that day.

At Love God Greatly, we use the SOAP Bible study method. Before beginning, let's take a moment to define this method and share why we recommend using it during your quiet time in the following pages.

The most important ingredients in the Soap method are your interaction with God's Word and your application of His Word to your life.

It's one thing to simply read Scripture. But when you interact with it, intentionally slowing down to really reflect on it, suddenly words start popping off the page. The SOAP method allows you to dig deeper into Scripture and see more than you would if you simply read the verses and then went on your merry way.

The most important ingredients in the SOAP method are your interaction with God's Word and your application of His Word to your life:

Blessed is the one who does not walk in step with the wicked or stand in the way that sinners take or sit in the company of mockers, but whose delight is in the law of the LORD, and who meditates on his law day and night. That person is like a tree planted by streams of water, which yields its fruit in season and whose leaf does not wither— whatever they do prospers.
(Ps. 1:1–3, NIV)

Please take the time to SOAP through our Bible studies and see for yourself how much more you get from your daily reading.

You'll be amazed.

SOAP STUDY *(CONTINUED)*

WHAT DOES SOAP MEAN?

S STANDS FOR
SCRIPTURE

*Physically write out the
verses.*

*You'll be amazed at what
God will reveal to you
just by taking the time to
slow down and write out
what you are reading!*

MONDAY

READ
Colossians 1:5–8

SOAP
Colossians 1:5–8

Scripture

WRITE
OUT THE
SCRIPTURE
PASSAGE
FOR THE
DAY.

The faith and love that spring from the hope stored up for you in heaven and about which you have already heard in the true message of the gospel that has come to you. In the same way the gospel is bearing fruit and growing throughout the whole world just as it has been doing among you since the day you heard it and truly understood God's grace. You learned it from Epaphras, our dear fellow servant, who is a faithful minister of Christ on our behalf, and who also told us of your love in the Spirit.

Observations

WRITE
DOWN 1 OR 2
OBSERVATIONS
FROM THE
PASSAGE.

When you combine faith and love, you get hope. We must remember that our hope is in heaven; it is yet to come. The gospel is the Word of truth. The gospel is continually bearing fruit and growing from the first day to the last. It just takes one person to change a whole community Epaphras.

O STANDS FOR
OBSERVATION

*What do you see in
the verses that you're
reading?*

*Who is the intended
audience? Is there a
repetition of words?*

*What words stand out
to you?*

A STANDS FOR APPLICATION

This is when God's Word becomes personal.

What is God saying to you today?

How can you apply what you just read to your own personal life?

What changes do you need to make? Is there action you need to take?

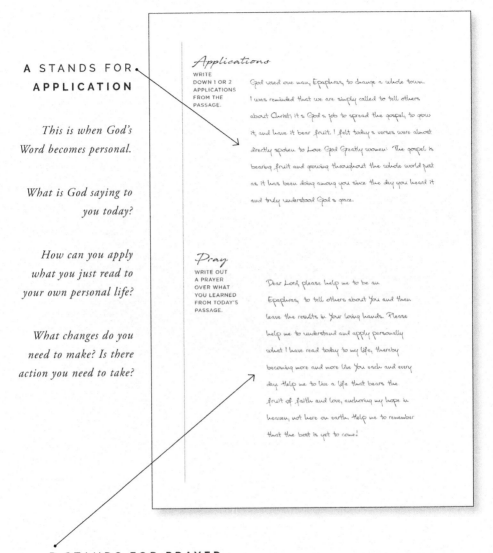

Applications

WRITE DOWN 1 OR 2 APPLICATIONS FROM THE PASSAGE.

God used one man, Epaphras, to change a whole town. I was reminded that we are simply called to tell others about Christ; it is God's job to spread the gospel, to grow it, and have it bear fruit. I felt today's verses were almost directly spoken to Love God Greatly women: "The gospel is bearing fruit and growing throughout the whole world just as it has been doing among you since the day you heard it and truly understood God's grace.

Pray

WRITE OUT A PRAYER OVER WHAT YOU LEARNED FROM TODAY'S PASSAGE.

Dear Lord, please help me to be an Epaphras, to tell others about You and then leave the results in Your loving hands. Please help me to understand and apply personally what I have read today to my life, thereby becoming more and more like You each and every day. Help me to live a life that bears the fruit of faith and love, anchoring my hope in heaven, not here on earth. Help me to remember that the best is yet to come!

P STANDS FOR PRAYER

Pray God's Word back to Him. Spend time thanking Him.

If He has revealed something to you during this time in His Word, pray about it.

If He has revealed some sin that is in your life, confess. And remember, He loves you dearly.

A RECIPE FOR YOU

COLOMBIAN BEEF EMPANADA

1. Dough or Masa

1 ½ cups precooked masarepa

2 cups water

1 tablespoon vegetable oil

½ tablespoon sazon Goya with azafran or food colouring

½ teaspoon Salt

2. Filling

1 Lb. peeled and diced white potatoes (around 3-4 potatoes)

1 tablespoon olive oil

¼ cup chopped white onions

¼ cup chopped green onions

1 cup chopped tomato

½ teaspoon salt

½ teaspoon adobo

¼ cup chopped green onions

1 chopped garlic clove

2 tablespoon chopped red bell pepper

1 Lb. minced beef (or pork)

Directions

- To prepare the dough; Place the masarepa in a large bowl. Add the sazon Goya with azafran and salt and stir to mix well. Add the water and oil and mix to form dough. Pat the dough into a ball and knead for 2 minutes or until smooth. Cover with plastic and set aside for 10 minutes.

- Meanwhile, to make the filling, cook the potatoes in a pot with water and the salt for 20-25 minutes or until tender. Drain and gently mash the potatoes. Set aside.

- Heat 1 tablespoon olive oil in a large, heavy skillet. Add the onion and cook over medium-low heat stirring frequently, for 5 minutes. Add the tomatoes, green onions, garlic, bell pepper, salt. Cook for about 15 minutes.

- Add the ground beef or pork. Cook, breaking up the meat with a wooden spoon, for 10 to 15 minutes or until the mixture is fairly dry.

- Transfer the meat mixture to the mashed potatoes bowl and mix well to combine.

- Break small portions of the dough, about 1 ½ tablespoons each one, and form each portion into a ball by rolling between the palms of your hands.

- Place the balls of dough between two pieces of plastic and roll each out very thinly to form a circle. Remove the top plastic and place 1 tablespoon of the filling in the center of each.

- Then using the plastic underneath, fold the dough over to enclose the filling, forming a half circle. Tightly seal the edges by crimping with the tines of a fork.

- Fill a large pot with vegetable oil and heat over medium heat to 360° F.

- Carefully place 3 or 4 empanadas at the time in the heated oil and fry for about 3 -4 minutes until golden on all sides.

- Using a slotted spoon transfer the empanadas to a plate lined with paper towels. Serve with aji and lime on the side.

1 & 2

TIMOTHY

Living Out the Gospel

Let's Begin

INTRODUCTION

I & II TIMOTHY

Paul, formally a despiser of Christians, came face to face with Jesus on the road to Damascus and was radically changed. And this change led him to plant churches, go on missionary journeys, and write much of the New Testament. Two of the books he penned were letters written to a young man named Timothy.

Paul refers to Timothy as "my beloved child," indicating the possibility Paul led this young man to Christ or played an important role in his spiritual growth. Paul had fatherly affection for young Timothy and Timothy accompanied Paul on a number of his travels, ministering with him. After Paul was released from prison (Acts 28:30), he began a journey with Timothy revisiting a number of cities where he had preached. And when they arrived in Ephesus, Paul left Timothy behind in order for him to pastor a struggling church. These letters, I & II Timothy, were written to help Timothy lead the church in practical and theologically sound ways.

In I Timothy we'll find Paul charging Timothy to help sort out some issues this congregation was having, such as false teaching (1:3–7; 4:1–3; 6:3–5), materialism (6:6-19), the need for godly leadership (3:1–14), and disorderly worship (2:1–15).

II Timothy finds Paul back in a Roman prison for the second time (1:16; 2:9); however, he is not deterred from his mission. As Paul nears martyrdom, he passes the ministry torch to Timothy and exhorts him to continue the work by guarding the treasure of sound doctrine (1:14), remaining faithful in hardship (2:3-4; 3:10–12), and by standing firm and preaching the Word in the last days (3:15–4:5).

But these letters are also written to us, the followers of Christ today. Our study of I & II Timothy will teach us about the importance of a healthy, functional church that, according to God's standards, promotes gospel-centered teaching. A healthy church raises healthy believers, while churches weak in doctrinal preaching are theologically immature and apathetic to others' needs. These letters that Paul wrote to Timothy are meant for our instruction and growth in the knowledge of God's ways, as well as encouragement as we try to live godly lives and stand firm on His Truth in an ungodly world.

I & II Timothy are letters from one pastor to another, and yet these books remind us that all Scripture is God breathed and is useful for teaching, correction, and training in righteousness.

READING PLAN

WEEK 1
Instructions, Warnings and God's Grace

Monday
READ: I TIMOTHY 1:1-7 • SOAP: 1:5-7

Tuesday
READ: I TIMOTHY 1:8-11 • SOAP: 1:8

Wednesday
READ: I TIMOTHY 1:12-14 • SOAP: 1:13-14

Thursday
READ: I TIMOTHY 1:15-17 • SOAP: 1:15-16

Friday
READ: I TIMOTHY 1:18-20 • SOAP: 1:19

WEEK 2
Instructions for the church and deacons

Monday
READ: I TIMOTHY 2:1-7 • SOAP: 2:4-6

Tuesday
READ: I TIMOTHY 2:8-15 • SOAP: 2:8-10

Wednesday
READ: I TIMOTHY 3:1-7 • SOAP: 3:2 & 4

Thursday
READ: I TIMOTHY 3:8-13 • SOAP: 3:11-12

Friday
READ: I TIMOTHY 3:14-16 • SOAP: 3:15-16

WEEK 3
Instructions for living out our faith

Monday
READ: I TIMOTHY 4:1-8 • SOAP: 4:7-8

Tuesday
READ: I TIMOTHY 4:9-16 • SOAP: 4:9, 12, 16

Wednesday
READ: I TIMOTHY 5:1-10 • SOAP: 5:1-2, 4

Thursday
READ: I TIMOTHY 5:11-16 • SOAP: 5:14-16

Friday
READ: I TIMOTHY 5:17-25 • SOAP: 5:18-19

READING PLAN *(CONTINUED)*

WEEK 4
Instructions on how to use money for God's glory

Monday
READ: I TIMOTHY 6:1-2 • SOAP: 6:2

Tuesday
READ: I TIMOTHY 6:3-10 • SOAP: 6:6-7, 10

Wednesday
READ: I TIMOTHY 6:11-16 • SOAP: 6:11-12

Thursday
READ: I TIMOTHY 6:17-19 • SOAP: 6:18-19

Friday
READ: I TIMOTHY 6:20-21 • SOAP: 6:20-21

WEEK 5
We are called to be faithful

Monday
READ: 2 TIMOTHY 1:1-71 • SOAP: 1:7

Tuesday
READ: 2 TIMOTHY 1:8-18 • SOAP: 1:8-9,13-14

Wednesday
READ: 2 TIMOTHY 2:1-13 • SOAP: 2:8-10

Thursday
READ: 2 TIMOTHY 2:14-19 • SOAP: 2:14-15

Friday
READ: 2 TIMOTHY 2:20-26 • SOAP: 2:23-26

WEEK 6
We are called to encourage the next generation

Monday
READ: 2 TIMOTHY 3:1-9 • SOAP: 3:2-5

Tuesday
READ: 2 TIMOTHY 3:10-17 • SOAP: 3:16-17

Wednesday
READ: 2 TIMOTHY 4:1-5 • SOAP: 4:2-4

Thursday
READ: 2 TIMOTHY 4:6-8 • SOAP: 4:7

Friday
READ: 2 TIMOTHY 4:9-22 • SOAP: 4:17-18

YOUR GOALS

WE BELIEVE it's important to write out goals for this study. Take some time now and write three goals you would like to focus on as you begin to rise each day and dig into God's Word. Make sure and refer back to these goals throughout the next six weeks to help you stay focused. You can do it!

1.

2.

3.

Signature:

Date:

WEEK 1

---

*And the grace
of our Lord overflowed
for me with the faith
and love that are in
Christ Jesus.*

1 TIMOTHY 1:14

CHALLENGE

Prayer focus for this week: Spend time praying for your family members.
Write down your prayer request and praises for each day.

You can find this listed in our Monday blog post.

MONDAY

TUESDAY

WEDNESDAY

THURSDAY

FRIDAY

MONDAY

Scripture for Week 1

1 Timothy 1:1-7

1 Paul, an apostle of Christ Jesus by command of God our Savior and of Christ Jesus our hope,

2 To Timothy, my true child in the faith:
Grace, mercy, and peace from God the Father and Christ Jesus our Lord.

3 As I urged you when I was going to Macedonia, remain at Ephesus so that you may charge certain persons not to teach any different doctrine, 4 nor to devote themselves to myths and endless genealogies, which promote speculations rather than the stewardship from God that is by faith. 5 The aim of our charge is love that issues from a pure heart and a good conscience and a sincere faith. 6 Certain persons, by swerving from these, have wandered away into vain discussion, 7 desiring to be teachers of the law, without understanding either what they are saying or the things about which they make confident assertions.

MONDAY

READ
1 Timothy 1:1-7

SOAP
1 Timothy 1:5-7

Scripture

WRITE
OUT THE
SCRIPTURE
PASSAGE
FOR THE
DAY.

Observations

WRITE
DOWN 1 OR 2
OBSERVATIONS
FROM THE
PASSAGE.

Applications

WRITE
DOWN 1 OR 2
APPLICATIONS
FROM THE
PASSAGE.

Pray

WRITE OUT
A PRAYER
OVER WHAT
YOU LEARNED
FROM TODAY'S
PASSAGE.

TUESDAY
Scripture for Week 1

1 Timothy 1:8-11

8 Now we know that the law is good, if one uses it lawfully, 9 understanding this, that the law is not laid down for the just but for the lawless and disobedient, for the ungodly and sinners, for the unholy and profane, for those who strike their fathers and mothers, for murderers, 10 the sexually immoral, men who practice homosexuality, enslavers, liars, perjurers, and whatever else is contrary to sound doctrine, 11 in accordance with the gospel of the glory of the blessed God with which I have been entrusted.

TUESDAY

READ
1 Timothy 1:8-11

SOAP
1 Timothy 1:8

Scripture

WRITE
OUT THE
SCRIPTURE
PASSAGE
FOR THE
DAY.

Observations

WRITE
DOWN 1 OR 2
OBSERVATIONS
FROM THE
PASSAGE.

Applications

WRITE
DOWN 1 OR 2
APPLICATIONS
FROM THE
PASSAGE.

Pray

WRITE OUT
A PRAYER
OVER WHAT
YOU LEARNED
FROM TODAY'S
PASSAGE.

WEDNESDAY
Scripture for Week 1

1 Timothy 1:12-14

12 I thank him who has given me strength, Christ Jesus our Lord, because he judged me faithful, appointing me to his service, 13 though formerly I was a blasphemer, persecutor, and insolent opponent. But I received mercy because I had acted ignorantly in unbelief, 14 and the grace of our Lord overflowed for me with the faith and love that are in Christ Jesus.

WEDNESDAY

READ
1 Timothy 1:12-14

SOAP
1 Timothy 1:13-14

Scripture

WRITE
OUT THE
SCRIPTURE
PASSAGE
FOR THE
DAY.

Observations

WRITE
DOWN 1 OR 2
OBSERVATIONS
FROM THE
PASSAGE.

Applications

WRITE
DOWN 1 OR 2
APPLICATIONS
FROM THE
PASSAGE.

Pray

WRITE OUT
A PRAYER
OVER WHAT
YOU LEARNED
FROM TODAY'S
PASSAGE.

THURSDAY

Scripture for Week 1

1 Timothy 1:15-17

15 The saying is trustworthy and deserving of full
acceptance, that Christ Jesus came into the world to save
sinners, of whom I am the foremost. 16 But I received
mercy for this reason, that in me, as the foremost,
Jesus Christ might display his perfect patience as an
example to those who were to believe in him for eternal
life. 17 To the King of the ages, immortal, invisible, the
only God, be honor and glory forever and ever. Amen.

THURSDAY

READ
1 Timothy 1:15-17

SOAP
1 Timothy 1:15-16

Scripture

WRITE
OUT THE
SCRIPTURE
PASSAGE
FOR THE
DAY.

Observations

WRITE
DOWN 1 OR 2
OBSERVATIONS
FROM THE
PASSAGE.

Applications

WRITE
DOWN 1 OR 2
APPLICATIONS
FROM THE
PASSAGE.

Pray

WRITE OUT
A PRAYER
OVER WHAT
YOU LEARNED
FROM TODAY'S
PASSAGE.

FRIDAY

Scripture for Week 1

1 Timothy 1:18-20

18 This charge I entrust to you, Timothy, my child,
in accordance with the prophecies previously made
about you, that by them you may wage the good
warfare, 19 holding faith and a good conscience. By
rejecting this, some have made shipwreck of their
faith, 20 among whom are Hymenaeus and Alexander,
whom I have handed over to Satan that they may learn
not to blaspheme.

FRIDAY

READ
1 Timothy 1:18-20

SOAP
1 Timothy 1:19

Scripture

WRITE
OUT THE
SCRIPTURE
PASSAGE
FOR THE
DAY.

Observations

WRITE
DOWN 1 OR 2
OBSERVATIONS
FROM THE
PASSAGE.

Applications

WRITE
DOWN 1 OR 2
APPLICATIONS
FROM THE
PASSAGE.

Pray

WRITE OUT
A PRAYER
OVER WHAT
YOU LEARNED
FROM TODAY'S
PASSAGE.

REFLECTION
QUESTIONS

1. According to v5, what is Paul's goal for Timothy?

2. What necessary quality is lacking in some people who want to be teachers? *(Think: Why is this a problem, and what consequences may come as a result?)*

3. What is meant by "sound doctrine" (v10)?

4. What is meant by the "gospel" (v11)?

5. Name three characteristics of God listed in v17 and explain a little about each one.

NOTES

WEEK 2

---

*For there is
one God, and there is
one mediator between
God and men, the man
Christ Jesus.*

1 TIMOTHY 2:5

CHALLENGE

Prayer focus for this week: Spend time praying for your country.
Write down your prayer request and praises for each day.

You can find this listed in our Monday blog post.

MONDAY

TUESDAY

WEDNESDAY

THURSDAY

FRIDAY

MONDAY

Scripture for Week 2

1 Timothy 2:1-7

1First of all, then, I urge that supplications, prayers, intercessions, and thanksgivings be made for all people, 2 for kings and all who are in high positions, that we may lead a peaceful and quiet life, godly and dignified in every way. 3 This is good, and it is pleasing in the sight of God our Savior, 4 who desires all people to be saved and to come to the knowledge of the truth. 5 For there is one God, and there is one mediator between God and men, the man Christ Jesus, 6 who gave himself as a ransom for all, which is the testimony given at the proper time. 7 For this I was appointed a preacher and an apostle (I am telling the truth, I am not lying), a teacher of the Gentiles in faith and truth.

MONDAY

READ
1 Timothy 2:1-7

SOAP
1 Timothy 2:4-6

Scripture

WRITE
OUT THE
SCRIPTURE
PASSAGE
FOR THE
DAY.

Observations

WRITE
DOWN 1 OR 2
OBSERVATIONS
FROM THE
PASSAGE.

Applications

WRITE
DOWN 1 OR 2
APPLICATIONS
FROM THE
PASSAGE.

Pray

WRITE OUT
A PRAYER
OVER WHAT
YOU LEARNED
FROM TODAY'S
PASSAGE.

TUESDAY

Scripture for Week 2

1 Timothy 2:8-15

8 I desire then that in every place the men should pray, lifting holy hands without anger or quarreling; 9 likewise also that women should adorn themselves in respectable apparel, with modesty and self-control, not with braided hair and gold or pearls or costly attire, 10 but with what is proper for women who profess godliness—with good works. 11 Let a woman learn quietly with all submissiveness.12 I do not permit a woman to teach or to exercise authority over a man; rather, she is to remain quiet. 13 For Adam was formed first, then Eve; 14 and Adam was not deceived, but the woman was deceived and became a transgressor. 15 Yet she will be saved through childbearing—if they continue in faith and love and holiness, with self-control.

T U E S D A Y

READ
1 Timothy 2:8-15

SOAP
1 Timothy 2:8-10

Scripture

WRITE
OUT THE
SCRIPTURE
PASSAGE
FOR THE
DAY.

Observations

WRITE
DOWN 1 OR 2
OBSERVATIONS
FROM THE
PASSAGE.

Applications

WRITE
DOWN 1 OR 2
APPLICATIONS
FROM THE
PASSAGE.

Pray

WRITE OUT
A PRAYER
OVER WHAT
YOU LEARNED
FROM TODAY'S
PASSAGE.

WEDNESDAY

1 Timothy 3:1-7

1The saying is trustworthy: If anyone aspires to the
office of overseer, he desires a noble task. 2 Therefore an
overseer must be above reproach, the husband
of one wife, sober-minded, self-controlled,
respectable, hospitable, able to teach, 3 not a drunkard,
not violent but gentle, not quarrelsome, not a lover
of money. 4 He must manage his own household well,
with all dignity keeping his children submissive, 5 for
if someone does not know how to manage his own
household, how will he care for God's church? 6 He must
not be a recent convert, or he may become puffed up
with conceit and fall into the condemnation of the devil.
7 Moreover, he must be well thought of by outsiders,
so that he may not fall into disgrace, into a snare of the
devil.

WEDNESDAY

READ
1 Timothy 3:1-7

SOAP
1 Timothy 3:2 & 4

Scripture

WRITE
OUT THE
SCRIPTURE
PASSAGE
FOR THE
DAY.

Observations

WRITE
DOWN 1 OR 2
OBSERVATIONS
FROM THE
PASSAGE.

Applications

WRITE
DOWN 1 OR 2
APPLICATIONS
FROM THE
PASSAGE.

Pray

WRITE OUT
A PRAYER
OVER WHAT
YOU LEARNED
FROM TODAY'S
PASSAGE.

THURSDAY

Scripture for Week 2

1 Timothy 3:8-13

8 Deacons likewise must be dignified, not double-tongued, not addicted to much wine, not greedy for dishonest gain. 9 They must hold the mystery of the faith with a clear conscience. 10 And let them also be tested first; then let them serve as deacons if they prove themselves blameless. 11 Their wives likewise must be dignified, not slanderers, but sober-minded, faithful in all things. 12 Let deacons each be the husband of one wife, managing their children and their own households well. 13 For those who serve well as deacons gain a good standing for themselves and also great confidence in the faith that is in Christ Jesus.

THURSDAY

READ
1 Timothy 3:8-13

SOAP
1 Timothy 3:11-12

Scripture

WRITE
OUT THE
SCRIPTURE
PASSAGE
FOR THE
DAY.

Observations

WRITE
DOWN 1 OR 2
OBSERVATIONS
FROM THE
PASSAGE.

Applications

WRITE
DOWN 1 OR 2
APPLICATIONS
FROM THE
PASSAGE.

Pray

WRITE OUT
A PRAYER
OVER WHAT
YOU LEARNED
FROM TODAY'S
PASSAGE.

FRIDAY

Scripture for Week 2

1 Timothy 3:14-16

14 I hope to come to you soon, but I am writing these
things to you so that, 15 if I delay, you may know how
one ought to behave in the household of God, which
is the church of the living God, a pillar and buttress of
the truth. 16 Great indeed, we confess, is the mystery of
godliness:

He was manifested in the flesh,
    vindicated by the Spirit,
        seen by angels,
proclaimed among the nations,
    believed on in the world,
        taken up in glory.

FRIDAY

READ
1 Timothy 3:14-16

SOAP
1 Timothy 3:15-16

Scripture

WRITE
OUT THE
SCRIPTURE
PASSAGE
FOR THE
DAY.

Observations

WRITE
DOWN 1 OR 2
OBSERVATIONS
FROM THE
PASSAGE.

Applications

WRITE
DOWN 1 OR 2
APPLICATIONS
FROM THE
PASSAGE.

Pray

WRITE OUT
A PRAYER
OVER WHAT
YOU LEARNED
FROM TODAY'S
PASSAGE.

REFLECTION QUESTIONS

1. Who, specifically, should we pray for and why?

2. What should a woman's focus be?

3. What is an "elder" or "overseer" and what are their qualifications?

4. What is a "deacon" and what are their qualifications?

5. Why is it important to manage your household well?

NOTES

WEEK 3

---

*For while bodily
training is of some value,
godliness is of value in every
way, as it holds promise
for the present life and also
for the life to come.*

1 TIMOTHY 4:8

CHALLENGE

Prayer focus for this week: Spend time praying for your friends.
Write down your prayer request and praises for each day.

You can find this listed in our Monday blog post.

MONDAY

TUESDAY

WEDNESDAY

THURSDAY

FRIDAY

MONDAY

Scripture for Week 3

1 Timothy 4:1-8

1Now the Spirit expressly says that in later times some
will depart from the faith by devoting themselves
to deceitful spirits and teachings of demons, 2 through
the insincerity of liars whose consciences are
seared, 3 who forbid marriage and require abstinence
from foods that God created to be received with
thanksgiving by those who believe and know the
truth. 4 For everything created by God is good,
and nothing is to be rejected if it is received with
thanksgiving, 5 for it is made holy by the word of God
and prayer.

6 If you put these things before the brothers, you will
be a good servant of Christ Jesus, being trained in the
words of the faith and of the good doctrine that you
have followed. 7 Have nothing to do with irreverent, silly
myths. Rather train yourself for godliness; 8 for
while bodily training is of some value, godliness is of
value in every way, as it holds promise for the present life
and also for the life to come.

MONDAY

READ
1 Timothy 4:1-8

SOAP
1 Timothy 4:7-8

Scripture

WRITE
OUT THE
SCRIPTURE
PASSAGE
FOR THE
DAY.

Observations

WRITE
DOWN 1 OR 2
OBSERVATIONS
FROM THE
PASSAGE.

Applications

WRITE
DOWN 1 OR 2
APPLICATIONS
FROM THE
PASSAGE.

Pray

WRITE OUT
A PRAYER
OVER WHAT
YOU LEARNED
FROM TODAY'S
PASSAGE.

TUESDAY

Scripture for Week 3

1 Timothy 4:9-16

9 The saying is trustworthy and deserving of full acceptance. 10 For to this end we toil and strive, because we have our hope set on the living God, who is the Savior of all people, especially of those who believe.

11 Command and teach these things. 12 Let no one despise you for your youth, but set the believers an example in speech, in conduct, in love, in faith, in purity. 13 Until I come, devote yourself to the public reading of Scripture, to exhortation, to teaching. 14 Do not neglect the gift you have, which was given you by prophecy when the council of elders laid their hands on you. 15 Practice these things, immerse yourself in them, so that all may see your progress. 16 Keep a close watch on yourself and on the teaching. Persist in this, for by so doing you will save both yourself and your hearers.

TUESDAY

READ
1 Timothy 4:9-16

SOAP
1 Timothy 4:9, 12, 16

Scripture

WRITE
OUT THE
SCRIPTURE
PASSAGE
FOR THE
DAY.

Observations

WRITE
DOWN 1 OR 2
OBSERVATIONS
FROM THE
PASSAGE.

Applications

WRITE
DOWN 1 OR 2
APPLICATIONS
FROM THE
PASSAGE.

Pray

WRITE OUT
A PRAYER
OVER WHAT
YOU LEARNED
FROM TODAY'S
PASSAGE.

WEDNESDAY

Scripture for Week 3

1 Timothy 5:1-10

1 Do not rebuke an older man but encourage him as you would a father, younger men as brothers, 2 older women as mothers, younger women as sisters, in all purity.

3 Honor widows who are truly widows. 4 But if a widow has children or grandchildren, let them first learn to show godliness to their own household and to make some return to their parents, for this is pleasing in the sight of God. 5 She who is truly a widow, left all alone, has set her hope on God and continues in supplications and prayers night and day, 6 but she who is self-indulgent is dead even while she lives. 7 Command these things as well, so that they may be without reproach. 8 But if anyone does not provide for his relatives, and especially for members of his household, he has denied the faith and is worse than an unbeliever.

9 Let a widow be enrolled if she is not less than sixty years of age, having been the wife of one husband, 10 and having a reputation for good works: if she has brought up children, has shown hospitality, has washed the feet of the saints, has cared for the afflicted, and has devoted herself to every good work.

WEDNESDAY

READ
1 Timothy 5:1-10

SOAP
1 Timothy 5:1-2, 4

Scripture

WRITE
OUT THE
SCRIPTURE
PASSAGE
FOR THE
DAY.

Observations

WRITE
DOWN 1 OR 2
OBSERVATIONS
FROM THE
PASSAGE.

Applications

WRITE
DOWN 1 OR 2
APPLICATIONS
FROM THE
PASSAGE.

Pray

WRITE OUT
A PRAYER
OVER WHAT
YOU LEARNED
FROM TODAY'S
PASSAGE.

THURSDAY

Scripture for Week 3

1 Timothy 5:11-16

11 But refuse to enroll younger widows, for when their passions draw them away from Christ, they desire to marry 12 and so incur condemnation for having abandoned their former faith. 13 Besides that, they learn to be idlers, going about from house to house, and not only idlers, but also gossips and busybodies, saying what they should not. 14 So I would have younger widows marry, bear children, manage their households, and give the adversary no occasion for slander. 15 For some have already strayed after Satan. 16 If any believing woman has relatives who are widows, let her care for them. Let the church not be burdened, so that it may care for those who are truly widows.

THURSDAY

READ
1 Timothy 5:11-16

SOAP
1 Timothy 5:14-16

Scripture

WRITE
OUT THE
SCRIPTURE
PASSAGE
FOR THE
DAY.

Observations

WRITE
DOWN 1 OR 2
OBSERVATIONS
FROM THE
PASSAGE.

Applications

WRITE
DOWN 1 OR 2
APPLICATIONS
FROM THE
PASSAGE.

Pray

WRITE OUT
A PRAYER
OVER WHAT
YOU LEARNED
FROM TODAY'S
PASSAGE.

FRIDAY

Scripture for Week 3

1 Timothy 5:17-25

17 Let the elders who rule well be considered worthy
of double honor, especially those who labor in preaching
and teaching. 18 For the Scripture says, "You shall not
muzzle an ox when it treads out the grain," and, "The
laborer deserves his wages." 19 Do not admit a charge
against an elder except on the evidence of two or three
witnesses. 20 As for those who persist in sin, rebuke
them in the presence of all, so that the rest may stand in
fear. 21 In the presence of God and of Christ Jesus and of
the elect angels I charge you to keep these rules without
prejudging, doing nothing from partiality. 22 Do not be
hasty in the laying on of hands, nor take part in the sins
of others; keep yourself pure. 23 (No longer drink only
water, but use a little wine for the sake of your stomach
and your frequent ailments.) 24 The sins of some people
are conspicuous, going before them to judgment, but
the sins of others appear later. 25 So also good works are
conspicuous, and even those that are not cannot remain
hidden.

FRIDAY

READ
1 Timothy 5:17-25

SOAP
1 Timothy 5:18-19

Scripture

WRITE
OUT THE
SCRIPTURE
PASSAGE
FOR THE
DAY.

Observations

WRITE
DOWN 1 OR 2
OBSERVATIONS
FROM THE
PASSAGE.

Applications

WRITE DOWN 1 OR 2 APPLICATIONS FROM THE PASSAGE.

Pray

WRITE OUT A PRAYER OVER WHAT YOU LEARNED FROM TODAY'S PASSAGE.

REFLECTION QUESTIONS

1. In your own words explain what it means to have your "conscience seared with a hot iron" and how might this happen?

2. What did Timothy need to do to be a good minister (v6)?

3. What does v8 teach about bodily exercise vs. godliness? Is it okay to ignore our bodies? Why or why not?

4. Who should care for the widows?

5. How old must a widow be to be enrolled or taken into the number? What does "being enrolled" mean?

NOTES

WEEK 4

---

*But godliness
with contentment is great gain,
for we brought nothing
into the world, and we cannot
take anything out of
the world.*

1 TIMOTHY 6:6-7

CHALLENGE

Prayer focus for this week: Spend time praying for your church.
Write down your prayer request and praises for each day.

You can find this listed in our Monday blog post.

MONDAY

TUESDAY

WEDNESDAY

THURSDAY

FRIDAY

MONDAY

Scripture for Week 4

1 Timothy 6:1-2

1 Let all who are under a yoke as bondservants regard
their own masters as worthy of all honor, so that the
name of God and the teaching may not be reviled.
2 Those who have believing masters must not be
disrespectful on the ground that they are brothers; rather
they must serve all the better since those who benefit by
their good service are believers and beloved.

Teach and urge these things.

MONDAY

READ
1 Timothy 6:1-2

SOAP
1 Timothy 6:2

Scripture

WRITE
OUT THE
SCRIPTURE
PASSAGE
FOR THE
DAY.

Observations

WRITE
DOWN 1 OR 2
OBSERVATIONS
FROM THE
PASSAGE.

Applications

WRITE
DOWN 1 OR 2
APPLICATIONS
FROM THE
PASSAGE.

Pray

WRITE OUT
A PRAYER
OVER WHAT
YOU LEARNED
FROM TODAY'S
PASSAGE.

TUESDAY

Scripture for Week 4

1 Timothy 6:3-10

3 If anyone teaches a different doctrine and does not agree with the sound words of our Lord Jesus Christ and the teaching that accords with godliness, 4 he is puffed up with conceit and understands nothing. He has an unhealthy craving for controversy and for quarrels about words, which produce envy, dissension, slander, evil suspicions, 5 and constant friction among people who are depraved in mind and deprived of the truth, imagining that godliness is a means of gain. 6 But godliness with contentment is great gain, 7 for we brought nothing into the world, and we cannot take anything out of the world. 8 But if we have food and clothing, with these we will be content. 9 But those who desire to be rich fall into temptation, into a snare, into many senseless and harmful desires that plunge people into ruin and destruction. 10 For the love of money is a root of all kinds of evils. It is through this craving that some have wandered away from the faith and pierced themselves with many pangs.

TUESDAY

READ
1 Timothy 6:3-10

SOAP
1 Timothy 6:6-7, 10

Scripture

WRITE
OUT THE
SCRIPTURE
PASSAGE
FOR THE
DAY.

Observations

WRITE
DOWN 1 OR 2
OBSERVATIONS
FROM THE
PASSAGE.

Applications

WRITE
DOWN 1 OR 2
APPLICATIONS
FROM THE
PASSAGE.

Pray

WRITE OUT
A PRAYER
OVER WHAT
YOU LEARNED
FROM TODAY'S
PASSAGE.

WEDNESDAY

Scripture for Week 4

1 Timothy 6:11-16

11 But as for you, O man of God, flee these
things. Pursue righteousness, godliness, faith, love,
steadfastness, gentleness. 12 Fight the good fight of the
faith. Take hold of the eternal life to which you were
called and about which you made the good confession
in the presence of many witnesses. 13 I charge you in
the presence of God, who gives life to all things, and of
Christ Jesus, who in his testimony before Pontius Pilate
made the good confession, 14 to keep the commandment
unstained and free from reproach until the appearing
of our Lord Jesus Christ, 15 which he will display at
the proper time—he who is the blessed and only
Sovereign, the King of kings and Lord of lords, 16 who
alone has immortality, who dwells in unapproachable
light, whom no one has ever seen or can see. To him be
honor and eternal dominion. Amen.

WEDNESDAY

READ
1 Timothy 6:11-16

SOAP
1 Timothy 6:11-12

Scripture

WRITE
OUT THE
SCRIPTURE
PASSAGE
FOR THE
DAY.

Observations

WRITE
DOWN 1 OR 2
OBSERVATIONS
FROM THE
PASSAGE.

Applications

WRITE
DOWN 1 OR 2
APPLICATIONS
FROM THE
PASSAGE.

Pray

WRITE OUT
A PRAYER
OVER WHAT
YOU LEARNED
FROM TODAY'S
PASSAGE.

THURSDAY
Scripture for Week 4

1 Timothy 6:17-19

17 As for the rich in this present age, charge them not to be haughty, nor to set their hopes on the uncertainty of riches, but on God, who richly provides us with everything to enjoy. 18 They are to do good, to be rich in good works, to be generous and ready to share, 19 thus storing up treasure for themselves as a good foundation for the future, so that they may take hold of that which is truly life.

THURSDAY

READ
1 Timothy 6:17-19

SOAP
1 Timothy 6:18-19

Scripture

WRITE
OUT THE
SCRIPTURE
PASSAGE
FOR THE
DAY.

Observations

WRITE
DOWN 1 OR 2
OBSERVATIONS
FROM THE
PASSAGE.

Applications

WRITE
DOWN 1 OR 2
APPLICATIONS
FROM THE
PASSAGE.

Pray

WRITE OUT
A PRAYER
OVER WHAT
YOU LEARNED
FROM TODAY'S
PASSAGE.

FRIDAY

Scripture for Week 4

1 Timothy 6:20-21

20 O Timothy, guard the deposit entrusted to you. Avoid the irreverent babble and contradictions of what is falsely called "knowledge," 21 for by professing it some have swerved from the faith.

Grace be with you.

FRIDAY

READ
1 Timothy 6:20-21

SOAP
1 Timothy 6:20-21

Scripture

WRITE
OUT THE
SCRIPTURE
PASSAGE
FOR THE
DAY.

Observations

WRITE
DOWN 1 OR 2
OBSERVATIONS
FROM THE
PASSAGE.

Applications

WRITE
DOWN 1 OR 2
APPLICATIONS
FROM THE
PASSAGE.

Pray

WRITE OUT
A PRAYER
OVER WHAT
YOU LEARNED
FROM TODAY'S
PASSAGE.

REFLECTION
QUESTIONS

1. What problem did Paul again warn about in v3-5?

2. What is contentment?

3. In what ways is godliness gain?

4. Is money the root of all evil? Explain.

5. How do we win the good fight?

NOTES

WEEK 5

---

*For God gave us
a spirit not of fear but
of power and love and
self-control.*

2 TIMOTHY 1:7

CHALLENGE

Prayer focus for this week: Spend time praying for missionaries.
Write down your prayer request and praises for each day.

You can find this listed in our Monday blog post.

MONDAY

TUESDAY

WEDNESDAY

THURSDAY

FRIDAY

MONDAY
Scripture for Week 5

2 Timothy 1:1-7

1 Paul, an apostle of Christ Jesus by the will of God according to the promise of the life that is in Christ Jesus,

2 To Timothy, my beloved child:
Grace, mercy, and peace from God the Father and Christ Jesus our Lord.

3 I thank God whom I serve, as did my ancestors, with a clear conscience, as I remember you constantly in my prayers night and day. 4 As I remember your tears, I long to see you, that I may be filled with joy. 5 I am reminded of your sincere faith, a faith that dwelt first in your grandmother Lois and your mother Eunice and now, I am sure, dwells in you as well. 6 For this reason I remind you to fan into flame the gift of God, which is in you through the laying on of my hands, 7 for God gave us a spirit not of fear but of power and love and self-control.

MONDAY

READ
2 Timothy 1:1-7

SOAP
2 Timothy 1:7

Scripture

WRITE
OUT THE
SCRIPTURE
PASSAGE
FOR THE
DAY.

Observations

WRITE
DOWN 1 OR 2
OBSERVATIONS
FROM THE
PASSAGE.

Applications

WRITE
DOWN 1 OR 2
APPLICATIONS
FROM THE
PASSAGE.

Pray

WRITE OUT
A PRAYER
OVER WHAT
YOU LEARNED
FROM TODAY'S
PASSAGE.

TUESDAY

Scripture for Week 5

2 Timothy 1:8-18

8 Therefore do not be ashamed of the testimony about our Lord, nor of me his prisoner, but share in suffering for the gospel by the power of God, 9 who saved us and called us to a holy calling, not because of our works but because of his own purpose and grace, which he gave us in Christ Jesus before the ages began, 10 and which now has been manifested through the appearing of our Savior Christ Jesus, who abolished death and brought life and immortality to light through the gospel, 11 for which I was appointed a preacher and apostle and teacher, 12 which is why I suffer as I do. But I am not ashamed, for I know whom I have believed, and I am convinced that he is able to guard until that day what has been entrusted to me. 13 Follow the pattern of the sound words that you have heard from me, in the faith and love that are in Christ Jesus. 14 By the Holy Spirit who dwells within us, guard the good deposit entrusted to you.

15 You are aware that all who are in Asia turned away from me, among whom are Phygelus and Hermogenes. 16 May the Lord grant mercy to the household of Onesiphorus, for he often refreshed me and was not ashamed of my chains, 17 but when he arrived in Rome he searched for me earnestly and found me— 18 may the Lord grant him to find mercy from the Lord on that day!—and you well know all the service he rendered at Ephesus.

TUESDAY

READ
2 Timothy 1:8-18

SOAP
2 Timothy 1:8-9,13-14

Scripture

WRITE
OUT THE
SCRIPTURE
PASSAGE
FOR THE
DAY.

Observations

WRITE
DOWN 1 OR 2
OBSERVATIONS
FROM THE
PASSAGE.

Applications

WRITE
DOWN 1 OR 2
APPLICATIONS
FROM THE
PASSAGE.

Pray

WRITE OUT
A PRAYER
OVER WHAT
YOU LEARNED
FROM TODAY'S
PASSAGE.

WEDNESDAY

Scripture for Week 5

2 Timothy 2:1-13

1You then, my child, be strengthened by the grace that
is in Christ Jesus, 2 and what you have heard from me
in the presence of many witnesses entrust to faithful
men, who will be able to teach others also. 3 Share
in suffering as a good soldier of Christ Jesus. 4 No
soldier gets entangled in civilian pursuits, since his
aim is to please the one who enlisted him. 5 An athlete
is not crowned unless he competes according to the
rules. 6 It is the hard-working farmer who ought to have
the first share of the crops. 7 Think over what I say, for
the Lord will give you understanding in everything.

8 Remember Jesus Christ, risen from the dead,
the offspring of David, as preached in my gospel, 9 for
which I am suffering, bound with chains as a criminal.
But the word of God is not bound! 10 Therefore I endure
everything for the sake of the elect, that they also may
obtain the salvation that is in Christ Jesus with eternal
glory. 11 The saying is trustworthy, for:

If we have died with him, we will also live with him;
12 if we endure, we will also reign with him;
if we deny him, he also will deny us;

13 if we are faithless, he remains faithful—
for he cannot deny himself.

WEDNESDAY

READ
2 Timothy 2:1-13

SOAP
2 Timothy 2:8-10

Scripture

WRITE
OUT THE
SCRIPTURE
PASSAGE
FOR THE
DAY.

Observations

WRITE
DOWN 1 OR 2
OBSERVATIONS
FROM THE
PASSAGE.

Applications

WRITE
DOWN 1 OR 2
APPLICATIONS
FROM THE
PASSAGE.

Pray

WRITE OUT
A PRAYER
OVER WHAT
YOU LEARNED
FROM TODAY'S
PASSAGE.

THURSDAY

Scripture for Week 5

2 Timothy 2:14-19

14 Remind them of these things, and charge them
before God not to quarrel about words, which does no
good, but only ruins the hearers. 15 Do your best to
present yourself to God as one approved, a worker who
has no need to be ashamed, rightly handling the word
of truth. 16 But avoid irreverent babble, for it will lead
people into more and more ungodliness, 17 and their talk
will spread like gangrene. Among them are Hymenaeus
and Philetus, 18 who have swerved from the truth, saying
that the resurrection has already happened. They
are upsetting the faith of some. 19 But God's firm
foundation stands, bearing this seal: "The Lord knows
those who are his," and, "Let everyone who names the
name of the Lord depart from iniquity."

THURSDAY

READ
2 Timothy 2:14-19

SOAP
2 Timothy 2:14-15

Scripture

WRITE
OUT THE
SCRIPTURE
PASSAGE
FOR THE
DAY.

Observations

WRITE
DOWN 1 OR 2
OBSERVATIONS
FROM THE
PASSAGE.

Applications

WRITE
DOWN 1 OR 2
APPLICATIONS
FROM THE
PASSAGE.

Pray

WRITE OUT
A PRAYER
OVER WHAT
YOU LEARNED
FROM TODAY'S
PASSAGE.

FRIDAY

Scripture for Week 5

2 Timothy 2:20-26

20 Now in a great house there are not only vessels of gold and silver but also of wood and clay, some for honorable use, some for dishonorable. 21 Therefore, if anyone cleanses himself from what is dishonorable, he will be a vessel for honorable use, set apart as holy, useful to the master of the house, ready for every good work.

22 So flee youthful passions and pursue righteousness, faith, love, and peace, along with those who call on the Lord from a pure heart. 23 Have nothing to do with foolish, ignorant controversies; you know that they breed quarrels. 24 And the Lord's servant must not be quarrelsome but kind to everyone, able to teach, patiently enduring evil, 25 correcting his opponents with gentleness. God may perhaps grant them repentance leading to a knowledge of the truth, 26 and they may come to their senses and escape from the snare of the devil, after being captured by him to do his will.

FRIDAY

READ
2 Timothy 2:20-26

SOAP
2 Timothy 2:23-26

Scripture

WRITE
OUT THE
SCRIPTURE
PASSAGE
FOR THE
DAY.

Observations

WRITE
DOWN 1 OR 2
OBSERVATIONS
FROM THE
PASSAGE.

Applications

WRITE
DOWN 1 OR 2
APPLICATIONS
FROM THE
PASSAGE.

Pray

WRITE OUT
A PRAYER
OVER WHAT
YOU LEARNED
FROM TODAY'S
PASSAGE.

REFLECTION QUESTIONS

1. What kind of faith did Timothy have and where did he learn it from?

2. What are "sound words," and what is the "pattern" of sound words?

3. What hardships might soldiers face that are like what Christians face?

4. How do we "rightly handle the word of truth"?

5. Why are we told to avoid arguments?

NOTES

WEEK 6

---

*All Scripture is breathed
out by God and profitable for
teaching, for reproof,
for correction, and for training
in righteousness, that
the man of God may be
complete, equipped for every
good work.*

2 TIMOTHY 3:16-17

CHALLENGE

Prayer focus for this week: Spend time praying for you.
Write down your prayer request and praises for each day.

You can find this listed in our Monday blog post.

MONDAY

TUESDAY

WEDNESDAY

THURSDAY

FRIDAY

MONDAY

Scripture for Week 6

2 Timothy 3:1-9

1But understand this, that in the last days there
will come times of difficulty. 2 For people will
be lovers of self, lovers of money, proud, arrogant,
abusive, disobedient to their parents, ungrateful,
unholy, 3 heartless, unappeasable, slanderous, without
self-control, brutal, not loving good, 4 treacherous,
reckless, swollen with conceit, lovers of pleasure rather
than lovers of God, 5 having the appearance of godliness,
but denying its power. Avoid such people. 6 For among
them are those who creep into households and capture
weak women, burdened with sins and led astray by
various passions, 7 always learning and never able
to arrive at a knowledge of the truth. 8 Just as Jannes and
Jambres opposed Moses, so these men also oppose the
truth, men corrupted in mind and disqualified regarding
the faith. 9 But they will not get very far, for their folly
will be plain to all, as was that of those two men.

MONDAY

READ
2 Timothy 3:1-9

SOAP
2 Timothy 3:2-5

Scripture

WRITE
OUT THE
SCRIPTURE
PASSAGE
FOR THE
DAY.

Observations

WRITE
DOWN 1 OR 2
OBSERVATIONS
FROM THE
PASSAGE.

Applications

WRITE
DOWN 1 OR 2
APPLICATIONS
FROM THE
PASSAGE.

Pray

WRITE OUT
A PRAYER
OVER WHAT
YOU LEARNED
FROM TODAY'S
PASSAGE.

TUESDAY

Scripture for Week 6

2 Timothy 3:10-17

10 You, however, have followed my teaching, my conduct, my aim in life, my faith, my patience, my love, my steadfastness, 11 my persecutions and sufferings that happened to me at Antioch, at Iconium, and at Lystra— which persecutions I endured; yet from them all the Lord rescued me. 12 Indeed, all who desire to live a godly life in Christ Jesus will be persecuted, 13 while evil people and impostors will go on from bad to worse, deceiving and being deceived. 14 But as for you, continue in what you have learned and have firmly believed, knowing from whom you learned it 15 and how from childhood you have been acquainted with the sacred writings, which are able to make you wise for salvation through faith in Christ Jesus. 16 All Scripture is breathed out by God and profitable for teaching, for reproof, for correction, and for training in righteousness, 17 that the man of God may be complete, equipped for every good work.

TUESDAY

READ
2 Timothy 3:10-17

SOAP
2 Timothy 3:16-17

Scripture

WRITE
OUT THE
SCRIPTURE
PASSAGE
FOR THE
DAY.

Observations

WRITE
DOWN 1 OR 2
OBSERVATIONS
FROM THE
PASSAGE.

Applications

WRITE
DOWN 1 OR 2
APPLICATIONS
FROM THE
PASSAGE.

Pray

WRITE OUT
A PRAYER
OVER WHAT
YOU LEARNED
FROM TODAY'S
PASSAGE.

WEDNESDAY

Scripture for Week 6

2 Timothy 4:1-5

1I charge you in the presence of God and of Christ
Jesus, who is to judge the living and the dead, and by his
appearing and his kingdom: 2 preach the word; be ready
in season and out of season; reprove, rebuke, and exhort,
with complete patience and teaching. 3 For the time is
coming when people will not endure sound teaching, but
having itching ears they will accumulate for themselves
teachers to suit their own passions, 4 and will turn
away from listening to the truth and wander off into
myths. 5 As for you, always be sober-minded, endure
suffering, do the work of an evangelist, fulfill your
ministry.

WEDNESDAY

READ
2 Timothy 4:1-5

SOAP
2 Timothy 4:2-4

Scripture

WRITE
OUT THE
SCRIPTURE
PASSAGE
FOR THE
DAY.

Observations

WRITE
DOWN 1 OR 2
OBSERVATIONS
FROM THE
PASSAGE.

Applications

WRITE
DOWN 1 OR 2
APPLICATIONS
FROM THE
PASSAGE.

Pray

WRITE OUT
A PRAYER
OVER WHAT
YOU LEARNED
FROM TODAY'S
PASSAGE.

THURSDAY

Scripture for Week 6

2 Timothy 4:6-8

6 For I am already being poured out as a drink offering, and the time of my departure has come. 7 I have fought the good fight, I have finished the race, I have kept the faith. 8 Henceforth there is laid up for me the crown of righteousness, which the Lord, the righteous judge, will award to me on that day, and not only to me but also to all who have loved his appearing.

THURSDAY

READ
2 Timothy 4:6-8

SOAP
2 Timothy 4:7

Scripture

WRITE
OUT THE
SCRIPTURE
PASSAGE
FOR THE
DAY.

Observations

WRITE
DOWN 1 OR 2
OBSERVATIONS
FROM THE
PASSAGE.

Applications

WRITE
DOWN 1 OR 2
APPLICATIONS
FROM THE
PASSAGE.

Pray

WRITE OUT
A PRAYER
OVER WHAT
YOU LEARNED
FROM TODAY'S
PASSAGE.

FRIDAY

Scripture for Week 6

2 Timothy 4:9-22

9 Do your best to come to me soon. 10 For Demas, in
love with this present world, has deserted me
and gone to Thessalonica. Crescens has gone to
Galatia, Titus to Dalmatia. 11 Luke alone is with
me. Get Mark and bring him with you, for he is very
useful to me for ministry. 12 Tychicus I have sent to
Ephesus. 13 When you come, bring the cloak that I
left with Carpus at Troas, also the books, and above
all the parchments. 14 Alexander the coppersmith did
me great harm; the Lord will repay him according to
his deeds. 15 Beware of him yourself, for he strongly
opposed our message. 16 At my first defense no one
came to stand by me, but all deserted me. May it not
be charged against them! 17 But the Lord stood by me
and strengthened me, so that through me the message
might be fully proclaimed and all the Gentiles might hear
it. So I was rescued from the lion's mouth. 18 The Lord
will rescue me from every evil deed and bring me safely
into his heavenly kingdom. To him be the glory forever
and ever. Amen.

19 Greet Prisca and Aquila, and the household of
Onesiphorus. 20 Erastus remained at Corinth, and I
left Trophimus, who was ill, at Miletus. 21 Do your best
to come before winter. Eubulus sends greetings to you, as
do Pudens and Linus and Claudia and all the brothers.

22 The Lord be with your spirit. Grace be with you.

FRIDAY

READ
2 Timothy 4:9-22

SOAP
2 Timothy 4:17-18

Scripture

WRITE
OUT THE
SCRIPTURE
PASSAGE
FOR THE
DAY.

Observations

WRITE
DOWN 1 OR 2
OBSERVATIONS
FROM THE
PASSAGE.

Applications

WRITE
DOWN 1 OR 2
APPLICATIONS
FROM THE
PASSAGE.

Pray

WRITE OUT
A PRAYER
OVER WHAT
YOU LEARNED
FROM TODAY'S
PASSAGE.

REFLECTION
QUESTIONS

1. What does Paul predict will happen in the last days? List the characteristics of people in those times (v2-5).

2. According to verse 12, all who follow the Lord will be persecuted. What does Paul mean?

3. What is the purpose of the scriptures (v17)?

4. What is meant by "in season and out of season"?

5. Paul ends the book by saying "grace be with you." What does that mean?

N O T E S

KNOW THESE TRUTHS
from God's Word

God loves you.
Even when you're feeling unworthy and like the world is stacked against you, God loves you - yes, you - and He has created you for great purpose.

God's Word says, "God so loved the world that He gave His one and only Son, Jesus, that whoever believes in Him shall not perish, but have eternal life" (John 3:16).

Our sin separates us from God.
We are all sinners by nature and by choice, and because of this we are separated from God, who is holy.

God's Word says, "All have sinned and fall short of the glory of God" (Romans 3:23).

Jesus died so that you might have life.
The consequence of sin is death, but your story doesn't have to end there! God's free gift of salvation is available to us because Jesus took the penalty for our sin when He died on the cross.

God's Word says, "For the wages of sin is death, but the free gift of God is eternal life in Christ Jesus our Lord" (Romans 6:23); "God demonstrates His own love toward us, in that while we were yet sinners, Christ died for us" (Romans 5:8).

Jesus lives!
Death could not hold Him, and three days after His body was placed in the tomb Jesus rose again, defeating sin and death forever! He lives today in heaven and is preparing a place in eternity for all who believe in Him.

God's Word says, "In my Father's house are many rooms. If it were not so, would I have told you that I go to prepare a place for you? And if I go and prepare a place for you, I will come again and will take you to myself, that where I am you may be also" (John 14:2-3).

Yes, you can KNOW that you are forgiven.
Accept Jesus as the only way to salvation...

Accepting Jesus as your Savior is not about what you can do, but rather about having faith in what Jesus has already done. It takes recognizing that you are a sinner, believing that Jesus died for your sins, and asking for forgiveness by placing your full trust in Jesus's work on the cross on your behalf.

God's Word says, "If you confess with your mouth that Jesus is Lord and believe in your heart that God raised him from the dead, you will be saved. For with the heart one believes and is justified, and with the mouth one confesses and is saved" (Romans 10:9-10).

Practically, what does that look like?
With a sincere heart, you can pray a simple prayer like this:

God,
I know that I am a sinner.
I don't want to live another day without embracing
the love and forgiveness that You have for me.
I ask for Your forgiveness.
I believe that You died for my sins and rose from the dead.
I surrender all that I am and ask You to be Lord of my life.
Help me to turn from my sin and follow You.
Teach me what it means to walk in freedom as I live under Your grace,
and help me to grow in Your ways as I seek to know You more.
Amen.

If you just prayed this prayer (or something similar in your own words), would you email us at info@lovegodgreatly.com?

We'd love to help get you started on this exciting journey as a child of God!

Love grows best in houses just like this

the natural home   Judith Wilson

THE KINFOLK TABLE

32

WELCOME, FRIEND. WE'RE SO GLAD YOU'RE HERE

Love God Greatly exists to inspire, encourage, and equip women all over the world to make God's Word a priority in their lives.

INSPIRE

women to make God's Word a priority in their daily lives through our Bible study resources.

ENCOURAGE

women in their daily walks with God through online community and personal accountability.

EQUIP

women to grow in their faith, so that they can effectively reach others for Christ.

Love God Greatly consists of a beautiful community of women who use a variety of technology platforms to keep each other accountable in God's Word.

We start with a simple Bible reading plan, but it doesn't stop there.

Some gather in homes and churches locally, while others connect online with women across the globe. Whatever the method, we lovingly lock arms and unite for this purpose...to Love God Greatly with our lives.

At Love God Greatly, you'll find real, authentic women. Women who are imperfect, yet forgiven. Women who desire less of us, and a whole lot more of Jesus. Women who long to know God through his Word, because we know that Truth transforms and sets us free. Women who are better together, saturated in God's Word and in community with one another.

Love God Greatly is a 501 (C) (3) non-profit organization. Funding for Love God Greatly comes through donations and proceeds from our online Bible study journals and books. LGG is committed to providing quality Bible study materials and believes finances should never get in the way of a woman being able to participate in one of our studies. All journals and translated journals are available to download for free from LoveGodGreatly.com for those who cannot afford to purchase them. Our journals and books are also available for sale on Amazon. Search for "Love God Greatly" to see all of our Bible study journals and books. 100% of proceeds go directly back into supporting Love God Greatly and helping us inspire, encourage and equip women all over the world with God's Word.

THANK YOU for partnering with us!

WHAT WE OFFER:

18 + Translations | Bible Reading Plans | Online Bible Study
Love God Greatly App | 80 + Countries Served
Bible Study Journals & Books | Community Groups

EACH LGG STUDY INCLUDES:

Three Devotional Corresponding Blog Posts | Monday Blog Videos
Memory Verses | Weekly Challenge | Weekly Reading Plan
Reflection Questions And More!

OTHER LOVE GOD GREATLY STUDIES INCLUDE:

David | Ecclesiastes | Growing Through Prayer | Names Of God
Galatians | Psalm 119 | 1st & 2nd Peter | Made For Community | Esther
The Road To Christmas | The Source Of Gratitude | You Are Loved

Visit us online at

LOVEGODGREATLY.COM

Made in the USA
Las Vegas, NV
25 September 2021